NATIVE AMERICAN PEOPLE

THE CROW

by Craig A. Doherty and Katherine M. Doherty

Illustrated by Richard Smolinski

ROURKE PUBLICATIONS, INC.

VERO BEACH, FLORIDA 32964

CONTENTS

Library of Congress Cataloging-in-Publication Data

Doherty, Katherine M.
    The Crow /by Katherine M. Doherty, Craig A. Doherty.
        p.   cm. — (Native American people)
    Includes bibliographical references.
    1. Crow Indians—Social life and customs—Juvenile literature. 2. Crow Indians—History—Juvenile literature.
I. Doherty, Craig A. II Title. III. Series.
E99.C92D64 1994   973'.04975—dc20   93-35660
    ISBN 0-86625-529-X   CIP
                                                            AC

Introduction

For many years, archaeologists—and other people who study early Native American cultures—agreed that the first humans to live in the Americas arrived about 11,500 years ago. These first Americans were believed to have been big-game hunters who lived by hunting the woolly mammoths and giant bison that inhabited the Ice Age plains of the Americas. This widely accepted theory also asserted that these first Americans crossed a land bridge linking Siberia, in Asia, to Alaska. This land bridge occurred when the accumulation of water in Ice Age glaciers lowered the level of the world's oceans.

In recent years, many scientists have challenged this theory. Although most agree that many big-game hunting bands left similar artifacts all over the Americas 11,500 years ago, many now suggest that the first Americans may have arrived as far back as 20,000 or even 50,000 years ago. There are those who think that some of these earliest Americans may have even come to the Americas by boat, working their way down the west coast of North America and South America.

In support of this theory, scientists who study language or genetics (the study of the inherited similarities and differences found in living things) believe that there may have been more than one period of migration. They

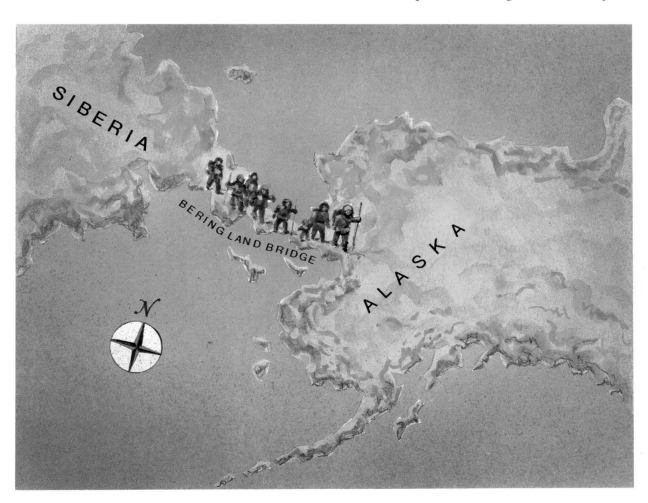

also believe that these multiple migrations started in different parts of Asia, which accounts for the genetic and language differences among the people of the Americas. Although it is still not certain when the first Americans arrived, scientists agree that today's Native Americans are descendants of early Asian immigrants.

Over the thousands of years between the first arrivals from Asia and the introduction of Europeans, the people who were living in the Americas flourished and inhabited every corner of the two continents. Native Americans lived above the Arctic Circle in the North to Tierra del Fuego at the tip of South America, and from the Atlantic Ocean in the East to the Pacific Ocean in the West.

During this time, the people of North America divided into hundreds of different groups. Each group adapted to the environment in which it lived. As agriculture developed and spread throughout the Americas, some people switched from being nomads to living in one area. Along the Mississippi River, in the Southwest, in Mexico, and in Peru, groups of Native Americans built large cities. In other areas, groups continued to exist as hunters and gatherers with no permanent settlements.

At least one group of Native Americans made the transition from settled farmers to nomadic hunters. The Hidatsa tribe lived in permanent farming villages in the Dakotas along the Missouri River. Some members of this tribe broke away and took up the lives of hunters, following the buffalo. These are the people called the Crow.

Origins of the Crow

Exactly when the Crow became a unique tribe is unknown. Clearly at one time they were part of the Hidatsa tribe. We know this from the

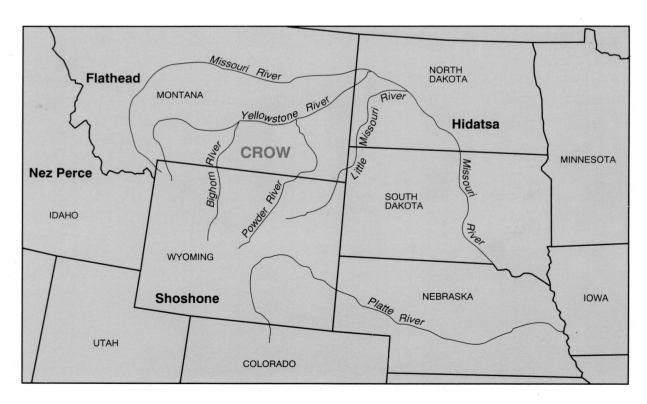

Crow's own stories and from the similarities in language; both tribes spoke a Siouan language. The Siouan languages were spoken by many tribes living between the Rocky Mountains and the Mississippi River.

The Hidatsa and the Crow were able to understand each other. Both tribes agreed that the Crow had once been part of the Hidatsa.

Some Hidatsa may have preferred the life of hunting on the plains. Food shortages among the corn-dependent Hidatsa also may have made the breaking away necessary. A significant number of Hidatsa moved west in order to follow the buffalo.

These Hidatsa became the Crow. The Crow are called Plains Indians. Most Plains Indians lived a nomadic life. They moved about a defined region following the patterns of the animals they hunted. For the Plains Indians, buffalo were the most important source of food and materials. As long as buffalo were plentiful, life was good for the Crow and the other Plains Indians.

The Pueblo Revolt of 1680, in New Mexico, provided horses left behind by the fleeing Spanish. Soon the Plains Indians were trading buffalo hides for horses. The horse increased the mobility of the Crow, who soon became excellent riders and breeders of horses.

The Crow consisted of two separate bands. The River Crow ranged along the lower Yellowstone River north to the Missouri River in what is now Montana. The Mountain Crow ranged farther south into the Big Horn and Wind River mountains in what is now the state of Wyoming. Although separate, they had similar customs and spoke the same language.

Daily Life

Native Americans had a variety of dwellings. In the Southwest, they built stone houses that were connected to form entire villages. In the Northeast, they built longhouses covered with bark. Each used the materials that were readily available. For the Crow and other Plains Indians, the most plentiful material was buffalo hides. With these, the Crow made *tipis* in which to live.

A *tipi* is often the type of shelter that is associated with Native Americans. The Crow *tipis* were made with a pole framework. The tallest poles were up to forty feet long. It took as many as twenty poles to make one *tipi*. Up to eight buffalo hides were usually sewn together to cover the framework. Certain women of the tribe were considered experts at making *tipi* covers.

When a family needed a new *tipi*, they would pay one of these expert women to help them. Up to twenty people often worked together to make the new *tipi* cover. The first task would be to prepare the thread to sew the hides together. Sinew (tendons) from buffalo and other game was used for this. Hides that had been previously treated were then cut. Once the treated hides were cut, they were sewn together to make a cover.

The hides were processed in a way that made them white. The Crow often decorated the inside of their *tipis*. The decorations were made with porcupine quills and paint. One side of the *tipi* might have shown an evil spirit, while the other depicted a good spirit. Often the accomplishments of the owner were painted on the outside.

Setting up a *tipi* was fairly easy, but it required teamwork. The four main poles were lashed together as they lay on the ground. One person separated the bottoms and then lifted the ends of the poles as high as possible. Another person would then pull them up, using a rope. Once these main poles were up, their bottoms were spread out and sharpened to penetrate the ground so they would not slip. The rest of the poles were then added.

After the pole frame was up, the *tipi* cover was stretched over it. Two poles were attached outside the *tipi* to flaps located at the peak. These poles were used to both open and close the flaps, depending on the weather. Crossbars were put on two of the poles to support the door. The crossbars were also used as a ladder to help raise the *tipi* cover. The top of the *tipi* was about twenty-five feet high. One early

European visitor among the Crow claimed that forty men could sit together for a meal inside a *tipi*.

It did not take long to raise or lower a *tipi*. This was fortunate, as the Crow moved as many as eight times during the summer months. In the winter, the Crow often chose a wooded and protected valley with a stream alongside it. Their *tipis* were usually set up among the trees. This provided some shelter from the harsh winter winds.

The cooking fire was built in the center of the *tipi*. The place of honor in a *tipi* was the side opposite the door. The Crow had no chairs, but they made backrests from willow branches and sinew that were supported by tripods. This made it comfortable to sit in the *tipi*. The Crow used buffalo robes and elkskin blankets to make their beds.

During the warmer months, the Crow built shade shelters next to their

Opposite: Members of a Crow village work together to set up their **tipis**. *Bottom: Smoke holes in the tops of tipis allowed the cooking fire to be set up inside.*

A painted Crow elkskin blanket.

tipis. When the weather allowed, they spent most of their days working under these shade structures. They were round, without walls, and had conical roofs made of boughs.

Family Life

Family life was significant to the Crow. They lived in small, nuclear-family units of a husband, wife, and their children. The Crow married at a very young age. It was not unusual for a girl to marry before she reached puberty. Boys married when they were in their midteens. After a brief courtship, a wedding ceremony was held.

The wedding ceremony consisted of the groom giving gifts to the bride's family. The groom's gifts usually consisted of horses, as they were the most valuable possessions of the Crow. After the gifts were given, the couple was considered married. When a couple first married, they often moved in with the groom's parents until they set up their own household.

Children were of great value to the Crow. All members of the tribe took responsibility for raising the children. Two days after a baby was born the mother would pierce his or her ears.

Shortly thereafter, the baby received his or her formal name. Often a Crow family asked an important member of the tribe to name their baby. Although the formal name of a child was significant, the Crow also used nicknames for their children.

Even though the Crow did not physically punish their children, they did have an interesting way to get children to stop crying. When children would cry, the parents would hold them upside down and pour water in their noses. Children quickly learned that crying was not accepted.

Infants were carried around on cradle boards that were a few feet long, about a foot wide, and tapered at the bottom. The Crow decorated their cradle boards with beadwork and attached a pouch in which to put the baby. Three straps secured the infant.

As soon as children were old enough, they began their education. For the Crow, this meant learning the skills that they would need as adults. Young

A Crow child is carried on her mother's back.

A Crow wedding ceremony.

boys were encouraged to hunt small game near their camps. Young girls helped their mothers butcher buffalo and prepare the skins.

Children were also instructed in their roles in clans, warrior societies, and various religious societies. Children were not usually given formal lessons. Instead, they learned by quietly watching their elders.

Food

The primary food of the Crow was meat, and most of it was buffalo meat. The fresh meat that the Crow ate was usually roasted over an open fire. Any meat that was not eaten fresh was dried for later use. The Crow had no

pots in which to cook. When they wanted to make soup or a stew, they used a boiling stone that had been heated in the fire. When the stone was very hot, it was put into a rawhide bag or bowl that contained the food they wanted to cook. The heat from the rock would cook the food without burning the container.

The Crow ate berries and roots that they collected in their hunting area. Corn was also a part of their diet. The corn that the Crow ate came from the Hidatsa. Since the Crow was once part of the Hidatsa tribe, they frequently traded with them.

The Crow did not grow crops for food, but they did grow small plots of tobacco. Sacred tobacco was an important aspect of their religious life.

A Crow woman prepares a meal over an open fire.

A Crow woman scrapes a buffalo hide to prepare it for use.

Hunting

Hunting was one of the most significant parts of life for the Crow. Their primary source of food, as well as their clothing and shelter, were dependent on hunting. Although the Crow were excellent individual hunters, the group buffalo hunts were crucial to the survival of the tribe.

The Crow had two main techniques for hunting buffalo, one that was developed before they had horses, and another one that was developed after. Before the introduction of the horse to the Plains Indians, the Crow used group drives in order to kill buffalo. During a group drive, the hunters would sneak in behind a group of buffalo. They would then start them moving toward a cliff. Sometimes rock fences were built to funnel the buffalo toward the kill site.

Other members of the tribe also took part in the group drive. They would wave their arms and blankets to scare the buffalo toward the cliff. In their panic, the buffalo would run off the cliff. If the cliff was high enough, the buffalo were killed by the fall. If the cliff was not high enough, more Crow hunters waited at the bottom, where they would kill the buffalo with their lances or bows. In this way, hundreds of buffalo were usually killed in a single drive.

A group hunt drives a herd of buffalo over the edge of a steep cliff.

Once the buffalo were killed, there was much more work to be done. The buffalo were then skinned and the hides were set aside for treating. Great quantities of meat were eaten in celebration of the successful hunt. As much as possible of the remaining meat was then dried and stored. The horns were removed and made into spoons, cups, and other utensils.

Once the Crow acquired horses, their hunting technique changed.

14

Crow hunters often disguised themselves as animals in order to stalk their prey.

They abandoned the group drives and began to hunt from their ponies. A group of mounted Crow hunters would circle a herd of buffalo and then lance or shoot them with a bow. Not as many buffalo were killed at one time, but the mobility of the hunters allowed them to travel and find more buffalo with greater ease.

The Crow also hunted deer, elk, antelope, and a variety of small game. This was done more for different types of hides and furs than necessity. Crow hunters were very good at stalking all their prey, including buffalo. They often wore a deer or coyote mask to sneak up on animals at watering holes. Although the Crow were accurate with their bows, they needed to get close to the animals to be effective.

Clothing

Appearance was important to both the Crow men and women. Their clothes were often highly decorated. A woman's best dress was usually made from either deerskin or mountain sheepskin. These dresses were long and covered a woman all the way from her neck down to her ankles. The main ornament on a dress was usually made from elk's teeth, accompanied by dyed

A Crow woman in traditional dress holds her infant.

porcupine quills. These beautifully decorated and colorfully embroidered dresses were sometimes trimmed with ermine fur.

The women wore their hair long, either left down or parted in the middle and braided. Perfumed bear grease was applied to their hair to give it shine and a nice fragrance. Both men and women used the scented bear grease on their hair.

All Crow wore the same footwear— buckskin moccasins. The Crow, who were excellent crafters of moccasins, could make their shoes from a single piece of buckskin. They frequently embroidered their moccasins with quills from a porcupine. Many people have said that the Crow did the finest beadwork of any Native American tribe in North America.

Today, some of the Crow fashion would be considered shocking. One description of Crow clothing states that the chiefs and other warriors usually decorated their clothing with the scalp locks of their enemies. The scalp locks were used as fringe on both sleeves and leggings. The Crow also made beautiful feathered warbonnets. This was a custom of other Plains Indians as well.

In addition to leggings and a shirt, the men wore a breechcloth and, in the winter, buffalo robes. Both men and women wore jewelry. Shells were often traded for and used in earrings, and bear claw necklaces were highly prized. When the Crow began trading with the Europeans for goods, they frequently traded for beads and metal jewelry. With these new materials, they created clothing that was even more ornate.

A Crow man, wearing a buffalo robe and feathered headdress, holds a war shield.

Games

The Crow played a variety of games, and most of these games had one thing in common: both the spectators and the participants gambled on them. Many of their games depended upon marksmanship skills. The Crow men had archery competitions with as many as one hundred participants. The winner kept the arrows that were used by all who competed.

The Crow also played a game that simulated hunting. A hoop with a net stretched across it was rolled along the ground. The men playing would then throw darts at the hoop. The one who could get his dart in the hoop was the winner. The Crow used counting sticks made from willow branches to keep track of the score.

Crow women were known to play a number of dice games. There appears to have been two main dice games. One was played with four marked sticks. The other was played using six pieces of bone or six plum pits.

The game with six dice was played by placing the dice in a bowl. The bowl was then hit on the ground, causing the dice to bounce. The object of the game was to get as many dice as possible flipped onto the same side. If all six were the same, the player was given six counting sticks. For other combinations, fewer sticks were given. The person with the most counting sticks at the end won the game.

A hand game was played by men and women together, in two teams of four or five players. Teams often competed for opponents' personal items, such as jewelry. A player from each team would start the game with one player holding an elk's tooth. With hands visible, he or she would switch the elk's tooth from hand to hand, much like a magician trying to fool the eyes of an audience. The other player would then try and guess in which hand the tooth was. A correct guess resulted in a counting stick for that team. The first team to get ahead by three counting sticks won.

Children, of course, also played games. Archaeologists have found miniature *tipis* at Crow campsites and believe that young children played with them, along with a variety of tops

Opposite: A Crow girl plays with her doll in a cradle board. Above: A group of children play dress-up in traditional adult clothing.

that were also found. In addition, Crow children played kicking games with balls. In the winter, the long rib-bones of buffalo were fastened tightly together and covered with a hide to make a sled. There was usually plenty of snow on the wintering grounds of the Crow.

The young boys of the tribe were often pitted against each other in competitive archery contests. Like their elders, the boys wagered with their arrows. Considering the fact that each arrow had to be carefully crafted by hand, these were extremely valuable prizes.

Horses and Dogs

Before the Crow acquired horses, the dog was their only domesticated animal. Dogs were very important to the Crow. Used to alert the village to danger, they also helped carry belongings from one campsite to the next. Before the Crow had horses, people's wealth was determined in part by how many dogs they owned.

The dogs were hooked to a travois, a kind of cart made of two poles tied together at one end. The tied end extended in front of the dog. Behind the dog, the poles would drag on the ground. A rectangular frame rested between the poles, and possessions of the dog's owner were then tied to the frame. Unlike some Native Americans,

A travois is loaded with supplies, which the dog will transport.

the Crow did not eat their dogs. Even after horses became the Crows' most valued possessions, dogs were still used to haul most Crow belongings.

Long before the Crow had encountered white people, they had horses. In 1680, the Pueblo Indians of New Mexico revolted against the Spanish who had settled in the Rio Grande Valley. The Spanish had tried to keep the Native Americans from acquiring horses. When the Pueblos revolted, the Spanish fled to Mexico, leaving their horses and a lot of other livestock behind. The Shoshone traded with the Pueblo Indians for horses. The Shoshone then traded them to the Crow and other Plains Indians. Along with horses, the Shoshone brought Spanish-style bits. A bit is the metal device that goes into the horse's mouth and gives the rider the ability to control the horse's direction.

The impact of the horse on the Plains Indians was great. The horse changed warfare among the Plains Indians, who then became some of

the most skilled cavalry in the world. The Crow and many other Plains groups spent much of their time raiding their enemies. Usually the object of their raids was to acquire horses.

In 1833, a European nobleman wrote of his visit to a Crow encampment at Fort Clarke, in what is now North Dakota. Near the fort there was a Hidatsa village, where the Crow had come to visit and trade. This nobleman learned that the Crow had about 1,200 warriors in their tribe and a total of 3,500 people. At this time, the Crow owned approximately 10,000 horses.

The introduction of the horse dramatically changed the Crow's way of life.

Political and Social Organization

The political organization of the Crow was linked to the social organization. The tribe was divided into two main groups—the Mountain Crow and the River Crow. The Mountain Crow were also divided into two groups. Anthropologists call a group within a tribe a band. Within each band, the Crow would break into camps of people who hunted together.

Among the Crow, everyone belonged to a clan. A clan is a group of families that claim a common ancestor in the distant past. There were as many as thirteen different Crow clans. The clans had distinctive names: Sor-lip clan, Without-shooting-they-bring-game clan, Greasy-inside-the-mouth clan, and others.

Clan membership was matrilineal, meaning that children became members of their mother's clan. People were expected to marry someone from outside their clan. Older members of a clan would take responsibility for teaching the children of their clan. Clan members also cooperated with each other during communal hunts.

In addition to being a member of a tribe, a band, and a clan, most men belonged to warrior societies. The warrior societies had names like Foxes, Muddy Hands, Lumpwoods, and Big Dogs. These groups had social, military, and political roles within the tribe.

The leaders of the warrior societies were also the leaders of the village. Leaders were selected because of their demonstrated achievements in battle. Before someone was selected as a leader, he had to prove himself by successfully leading a raid against one of the Crow enemies. He also had to take horses from within an enemy's camp. In addition, he had to steal an enemy's weapons and be the first to count coup in a battle. When a warrior got close to an enemy and tapped him without hurting him, it was considered a coup. Among the Crow and other Plains Indians, counting coup was believed to show more bravery than actually defeating the enemy.

Within the camps, the leaders of the warrior societies made decisions for the group. Each year, one of the warrior societies was selected to take the role of community police. They made sure that everyone worked together when they were moving or hunting.

Although there was not a single head of the whole Crow tribe, certain leaders gained more authority than others. They did this by being more accomplished as warriors. The camps and bands functioned separately, but when the territory of the Crow was threatened, all Crow might combine to attack an enemy. Normally, however, there were small independent raids on the part of the Crow and their enemies.

The Crow had both allies and enemies among the other tribes. The Hidatsa, along with the Mandan, were their main allies. At times, they traded with the Shoshone and the Blackfoot. But the Crow claimed a vast territory as their hunting grounds, and this caused them to have conflicts with most of the surrounding tribes. The Sioux, Cheyenne, Dakota, Blackfoot, and Shoshone all fought with the Crow from time to time.

A young Crow sets out on a vision quest.

Religious Life

For the Crow, as well as many other Native Americans, religion was a part of everyday life. There was very little separation between their everyday world and the spirit world.

The Crow believed that the world was created by a wise old coyote with the help of two ducks. One day, the coyote came upon the ducks, who were swimming in the ocean. He suggested that they dive down and see if there was anything on the bottom. After several attempts, one of the ducks brought up some mud. The coyote

took the mud and blew on it. When he did, the mud expanded, creating the land. One of the ducks suggested that the land would be more interesting if it had rivers and mountains. So the coyote created these. Then the coyote decided to create all the creatures to inhabit the earth.

The Crow also believed that their creator lived near them on the plains. Before going into battle, or on an important hunt, the Crow often went on vision quests. A Crow would go out onto the plains alone without food, in hopes of receiving a vision from the spirit world. A Crow might also cut

The Crow believed that a wise old coyote and two ducks created the world.

himself in an attempt to bring on a vision. These visions often involved an animal, especially a bear or a buffalo.

A Crow would frequently go on a vision quest before entering into battle. Young men would go on vision quests as they assumed the responsibilities of an adult. Interpreting the visions that someone had was important. Often the elders of the community were called upon to tell what a particular vision meant.

The Crow people believed in a life after death. They believed that the spirit of a dead person lingered for a period of time. After that time, the

24

spirit went to live in the camp of the dead. The body of a dead Crow was treated with respect. It was placed on a platform out on the prairie where the creator would find the spirit.

In the Crow religious observances the sun was a significant object, and one of their most important rituals was called the Sun Dance. The Sun Dance was performed irregularly, in an attempt for one or more warriors to seek a vision of revenge. If a Crow was killed in battle, the Sun Dance was held to determine how his fellow warriors would avenge his death. During the Sun Dance, the participants often tortured themselves. The Crow also worshipped the moon and tobacco.

Tobacco

Tobacco was the only crop the Crow grew, and it was grown for ceremonial purposes. Within the Crow tribe there was a Tobacco Society. It was the responsibility of the Tobacco Society to oversee the planting and care of the tobacco gardens. The Crow believed that tobacco seeds had originally been a gift to the Crow from the creator.

The planting of the sacred tobacco was an important ceremony each spring. Only special members of the Tobacco Society were allowed to prepare the seeds for planting. They mixed the seeds with water, ground bones, and animal dung before planting them.

Sacred tobacco was not smoked. However, tobacco for smoking was acquired through trade with other tribes. The Crow smoked this tobacco in long pipes on special occasions.

European Contact

The Crow were affected by Europeans long before they actually encountered any. At the end of the seventeenth century, the horse and the Spanish-style bit changed life on the plains for the Crow and other Plains Indians. It was not until 1805 that the Crow met a non-Indian. In that year, they met Francois Antoine Larocque, a French-Canadian, who was trading at a Hidatsa village when several Crow arrived for a visit. Larocque traveled with the Crow to see their home territory.

In 1806, the Lewis and Clark expedition passed through Crow territory without coming into contact with them. The next year, a member of that expedition, John Colter, went back to Crow territory. He and his partner, Manuel Lisa, set up a trading post that they called Fort Raymond. It was the first non-Indian dwelling in what is now the state of Montana.

By this time, the Crow had already acquired muskets from other Native

Two men share a peace pipe during a celebration.

Americans. They were eager to trade for more guns and other European goods. Metal tools and utensils made life easier for the Crow. Guns were mainly used in warfare, as the bow was still a more efficient hunting tool.

Horses and trade goods were not the only things of European origin that the Crow experienced before they had ever seen a non-Indian. European diseases, which had wiped out entire tribes in the East, struck the Crow in the eighteenth century.

By 1805, smallpox and other diseases had reduced the Crow from approximately 15,000 to 2,500 people. Five out of every six Crow had died from these European diseases.

In 1837, a group of Crow wintered at a Hidatsa village on the Knife River. The entire village was wiped out by smallpox. The Crow people were able to survive these epidemics in part because individual groups had limited contact with outsiders.

In the years immediately following the Civil War, many Americans wanted to leave the war-torn East. Thousands of people flooded the open spaces of the West. In 1868, the Crow signed a treaty with the U.S. government. In this treaty, they gave up over thirty million acres of land. In exchange for this, they received guarantees from the government that their remaining territory would be protected. The treaty also ensured that the Crow people would be allowed to hunt in any unoccupied areas of the plains.

The traditional life of the Crow rapidly ended. People using the new railroads swept westward and disrupted the life of the Plains Indians forever. Fences and plows further limited the

Medicine Crow was one of the chiefs to go to Washington, D.C., in 1880, as a Crow delegate.

land that was once open to the Crow. The most devastating blow to the Crow way of life was the near elimination of the buffalo herds. Non-Indian buffalo hunters swarmed into the plains and slaughtered the buffalo for their hides. At that time there was a market for them in the East and in Europe. Within a matter of years, the vast herds of buffalo were gone. Without the buffalo, the Crow found it extremely difficult to survive.

During this time, the Crow tried to remain neutral. Some Crow even worked as scouts for the army during their war against the other Plains Indians. The Crow were hoping to hold onto their lands by siding with the government.

This was when some members of the Crow tribe attempted to adjust their lifestyles. A number of Crow built permanent dwellings and took up farming. In 1880, six Crow chiefs were sent to Washington, D.C., and convinced to sign yet another treaty. Under this treaty, the government bought over one million acres of Crow

Opposite: In 1807, the Crow began trading with the Europeans at a post called Fort Raymond. Above: This ceremony was held to mark the last spike driven in the Northern Pacific Railroad, in 1883.

territory. The treaty also gave the railroad a 400-foot-wide right-of-way along the Yellowstone River. In addition, the Crow also agreed to be under the direction of a government-appointed agent.

The Native American agent for the Crow banned the Sun Dance. Some young Crow men who wanted to live in the traditional way participated in the Sun Dance of the Cheyenne. Many among the Crow supported these young men and their leader, Sword Bearer.

When rustlers stole Crow cattle, the government did nothing. Then a group of Blackfoot stole some horses. Sword Bearer and twenty-two of his followers retaliated. After a successful raid, they returned to their reservation and in celebration shot at the agent's house and store.

The government saw this as an uprising and hunted down Sword Bearer and his band. He and eight of his followers were killed. After this incident, the agent was more strict with the Crow.

Many Crow were forced to move out of the mountains and begin farming. At this time, the federal government passed the General Allotment Act of 1887, also known as the Dawes Act. The purpose of this law was to take all tribally held land in the United States and give it to individual Native Americans. Any tribal land remaining after this allotment would be sold. The writers of the law felt that individual land ownership would force Native Americans to become more like non-Indians.

In 1892, the government purchased another 1.8 million acres of Crow land. In 1904, the government secured even more Crow land. Under the Dawes Act, each adult Crow male was allotted 160 acres. In addition, he would get 80 acres for his wife and 40 acres for each child. For a people who had spent their lives traveling over hundreds of square miles, owning a few hundred acres was considered little compensation for the loss of their way of life.

In 1899, Crow children in school uniforms gather in front of the Pryor Boarding School in Montana.

The Crow Today

The Crow today suffer many of the same problems faced by other Native Americans. They want to hold onto their tribal identity but are almost forced to live in poverty to do so. At the time of the 1990 U.S. Census, there were 8,588 Crow. Over 6,000 Crow live in Montana, mainly on the Crow Reservation.

On the 2.2 million-acre Crow Reservation, the unemployment rate is over 80 percent. Among the Crow, alcohol-related deaths are eleven times the national average. Over half the reservation is leased to non-Indian ranchers or energy corporations. The Crow also have the sixty largest coal reserves in the world, but the depressed market for coal has caused a number of companies to back out of their leases.

On a more positive note, the Crow have held onto their language and culture. Three quarters of all Crow children are fluent in the Crow language. The Tobacco Society is still very active, as are other Crow religious traditions. Every August, since 1904, the Crow hold a tribal fair. The fair is a time of pride for the Crow. In 1982, Little Big Horn College opened on the reservation with twenty students. Today, hundreds of Crow students are enrolled in its programs.

The tribe is also politically active. The tribal government meets four times a year. All Crow over eighteen years old are allowed to vote in tribal elections. During the 1980s, the Crow won a discrimination case against the local county government and now have a member on the county board. Bill Yellowtail is a Crow who has been twice elected to the Montana State Senate.

Despite the problems they face, many Crow are optimistic. They seem to be coming to terms with the world outside their reservation. At the same time, improvements are happening within the reservation. Progress is slow, but there is hope that the Crow will be able to survive and prosper as a unique people within the framework of the mainstream culture.

Chronology

1680   Pueblo Revolt in New Mexico provides horses left behind by the fleeing Spanish.

1805   Francois Antoine Larocque, a French-Canadian, is the first non-Indian to meet the Crow.

1806   Lewis and Clark expedition passes through Crow territory without making any contact.

1807   John Colter and Manuel Lisa establish the first trading post in the Crow territory. It is called Fort Raymond.

1833   European nobleman visiting Crow encampment reports that Crow had approximately 3,500 people and 10,000 horses.

1837   A group of Crow spending the winter in a Hidatsa village are wiped out by smallpox.

1868   The Crow sign a treaty with the U.S. government. In the treaty, they give up claim to thirty million acres in exchange for the protection of their remaining land.

1876   Battle of the Little Big Horn is fought in Crow territory. Most Crow remain neutral.

1880   The Crow sign another treaty with the federal government, ceding more land to the United States.

1887   A group of Crow led by Sword Bearer attacks the Blackfoot, who had stolen some Crow horses.

        The General Allotment Act is passed, which gives tribal lands to individual Native Americans.

1892   The Federal government purchases another 1.8 million acres of Crow land.

1904   Crow land is allotted to individual tribal members. Crow hold first annual tribal fair.

1982   Little Big Horn College opens on Crow Reservation in Montana.

INDEX

Acknowledgments and Photo Credits
Cover and all artwork by Richard Smolinski.
P. 8: ©Blackbirch Press, Inc.; pp.11, 18, 19, 27, 29, 30: Smithsonian Institution/National Anthropological Archives.
Map by Blackbirch Graphics, Inc.